Come Holy Gift

I welcome this rich contribution to the growing revival of poetry for the Christian Calendar. Steven Shakespeare's deft and mellifluous poetry is in touch not only with the riches of Christian scripture and liturgy but also with the earlier creation spirituality of these islands, as the poems on Beltane and the Winter Solstice testify. He also brings a distinct Marian perspective to these poetic meditations, with his fine sonnets on the joyful, sorrowful, and glorious mysteries of the rosary tradition. This will be an excellent resource for any church whose liturgy follows the pattern of the Christian year.

Malcolm Guite, poet, priest and songwriter

Steven Shakespeare captures how poetry trembles on the threshold between presence and absence, opening the door to a prayerful participation in mystery. This is a profound and wonderful book, offering rich resources to accompany the year's worship and to deepen meditation, especially on the mysteries of the Rosary. It is for anyone who seeks to grow in the holy gift of grace. I heartily commend it.

Frances Ward, writer and former Dean of St Edmundsbury

'Poetic imagination' is at the heart of classic Anglicanism. That classic, catholic stream is in need of renewal and refreshment. Steven Shakespeare's work proves that we drink always at 'fresh springs'. Poetry and prayer are close relations. The poems in this collection demonstrate a sure hand in navigating the territory of the soul. Like the biblical psalms they have a rich complexity that will benefit from long reflection. The place of Mary as mother of Jesus and first believer will be attractive to many in reading these poems. They demonstrate that healthy piety, spirit of devotion and fundamental inclusiveness which has sustained catholic Anglicans for generations. Steven joins the great priest-poets of the Anglican tradition. This book is essential reading.

Richard Peers, Anglican priest and founding Superior of the Sodality of Mary

The prayer poems of *Come Holy Gift* call us to get 'out of our heads and ... into the flesh of our praying', putting our roots down deep into the rhythms of the liturgical year, the mysteries of incarnation and passion, and the Spirit-stirred undercurrents of creation itself. These are words that teach us to breathe.

Al Barrett, co-author of Being Interrupted

Also by the same author and available from Canterbury Press

The Earth Cries Glory: Daily Prayer with Creation Prayers for an Inclusive Church

Come Holy Gift

Prayer Poems for the Christian Year

Steven Shakespeare

CANTERBURY
PRESS
Norwich

Published in 2022 by Canterbury Press
Editorial office
3rd Floor, Invicta House,
108–114 Golden Lane,
London EC1Y OTG, UK
www.canterburypress.co.uk

Canterbury Press is an imprint of Hymns Ancient & Modern Ltd
(a registered charity)

Hymns Ancient & Modern® is a registered trademark of
Hymns Ancient & Modern Ltd
13A Hellesdon Park Road, Norwich,
Norfolk NR6 5DR, UK

Scripture quotations are from the New Revised Standard Version
Bible: Anglicised Catholic Edition, copyright © 1989, 1993, 1995
the Division of Christian Education of the National Council
of the Churches of Christ in the United States of America.
Used by permission. All rights reserved.

British Library Cataloguing in Publication data

A catalogue record for this book is available
from the British Library

ISBN: 978-1-78622-412-5

Typeset by Regent Typesetting
Printed and bound by
CPI Group (UK) Ltd

Contents

Part 3 Lent, Easter and Pentecost

Part 4 Transforming Ordinary Time

Part 5 In the School of Mary

Introduction

Prayer, poetry and sacrament

A sure way to kill poetry is to explain it to death. That said, the reader deserves a little context for the approach and structure of this collection.

One of the problems people often identify in Western Christian forms of worship is that they contain 'too many words'. On one level, I sympathize; where worship seems to demand that we grapple with multiple books and papers and high levels of literacy, it can appear exclusive, cerebral and alienating to those who do not know the language. It can leave too little space for silence or mystery.

Nevertheless, we should not be so quick to give up on words. It is true that words can often be debased: turned into units of currency, power, mere data. But words also have depth. They clear a space for encounter, light up the world, tremble on the threshold between presence and absence.

Those same Christian traditions which can be written off for their wordiness have, for all their faults, nurtured and handed on some of the most stunning, transformative language of human history. The Scriptures themselves are beautifully diverse, in ways which frustrate fundamentalist attempts to reduce them all to one level of absolute truth or falsity. To be a fundamentalist is not really to read the texts you use. This much is true of the so-called new atheists too. So much contemporary debate about religion is debate about a construct, a projection – and a lesson in how not to read.

When truly read, Scripture turns out to be a treasure hoard of myths, chronicles, heroic narratives, trickster tales, songs, poems, letters, visions, laws, dream sequences, proverbs, parables and more. This does not absolve Scripture of its contradictions or its texts of terror; but such problems only truly come alive when encountered in depth.

In worship, Scripture sings. The psalms in particular, but also such songs as the Magnificat or Benedictus, have been the cornerstone of rhythms of prayer and devotion since the earliest days of the Church. We might also think of the role Scripture has played in visionary and mystical experience (the love poems of the Song of Songs have been especially important here), or in contemplative and imaginative meditation (as in Ignatian prayer).

When we think of these examples, we soon arrive at a point where the boundaries between poetry and prayer become blurred. This collection is of 'prayer poems'. This is a title that might very well reflect my own imposter syndrome (How could I ever presume to write *proper* poetry?). However, it also contains a kernel of something important: the resonance between poetry and prayer.

Think about the well-known Carol Ann Duffy poem, which is itself simply called 'Prayer'.[1] It begins with the line, 'Some days, although we cannot pray, a prayer/utters itself.' It goes on to trace some experiences that, on the surface, are unremarkable, but which bear witness to a sense of depth and connection: a woman lifting her head at the 'singing' of a tree; a man remembering his youth in the 'distant Latin chanting of a train'. Simple piano scales, the calling of a name, the falling of darkness, the reciting of names on the Shipping Forecast: none of this is obviously religious, but it lights up a presence, a quality of 'thisness' in things which is more than any empirical observation or measurement could tell.

I think Duffy's poem suggests something true about prayer. It begins with a confession: that we cannot pray. How many of us have muttered something like that or heard it from others? And yet a prayer utters itself; the confession itself is a kind of prayer. There is a sense here that prayer is something more

---

1 'Prayer', from Carol Ann Duffy, *Mean Time*, London: Picador, 2013.

than the action of an individual, of an isolated ego in conscious charge of her own projects and plans. Prayer is something we are swept up in, a stream which emerges from subterranean caverns. We do not simply pray, we are prayed. Deep calls to deep, and – to allude to Romans 8 – the Spirit intercedes for us with sighs too deep for words.

I think poetry is a remembrance of prayer: it weaves together the underlying, stumbling connectedness of our half-formed prayers with the singing of creation itself, of things in their otherness. It is rooted in practices of attention, shaped by lament and desire. It works through the medium of words and spaces, which, like prayer, arise out of the creative depth of silence. Prayer and poetry are not just something we do, let alone something certain specially gifted individuals do; they are the atmosphere in which we live, breathe and communicate. From a Christian perspective, they are rooted in the living Word of God which calls creation into being out of silence.

For both poetry and prayer, silence is vital. The silence I mean is not emptiness, but awareness, a space for meeting and grace. John O'Donohue writes that 'The language of poetry issues from and returns to silence.'[2] Poetry lets the unsaid be heard. Not captured, but heard, and felt.

There is all the difference in the world between a silence that is alienating and one that is expectant, attentive; just as there is all the difference in the world between isolation or loneliness and the richness of solitude. Silence is necessary for our lives. It is the darkness, the depth out of which the word emerges, the word of prayer or the word of poetry, the word of recognition, greeting, connection. And ultimately, for Christians, our words are called out by the depth of our source, through the creative Word, in the life-giving Spirit. Poetry and prayer call us to pay attention to the echoing of God's word in ours, to our share in the unceasing, inexhaustible giving and receiving of love which is the triune God.

2 John O' Donohue, *Anam Cara: Spiritual Wisdom from the Celtic World*, London: Bantam, 1999, p. 143.

We need to remember that the centrality of poetry for Scripture is no accident. It is the living Word of God, which speaks in creation, which is made flesh in Jesus, which is expressed through Scripture. This Word can transform how we understand language itself.

The heart of the Word is a living expression and image of unceasing love: communication is this exchange of gifts. The Word is not just a tool, an idea or a show of force: he is the shaper of new being, the one who delights and suffers in human flesh. Connected with the figure of wisdom from the Hebrew Scriptures, she is present in all of creation. She is the one who guides and delights in the human race.

Poetry emerges from the silence of what is more than words, more than images; but which comes to inhabit and leave its trace upon our world. It is sensuous, embodied, resonant language. It is not vague, except by the measure of a very limited and narrow form of exactness; it holds a deeper question and a deeper precision. What it says cannot be said in other ways.

Rediscovering the rhythm of poetry and prayer is, I believe, core to an urgent demand of our time: what it means to think theologically about creation. Prayer – even the unsaid prayer of our faithlessness – is the offering of the creature back to the creator, the dark bridge between God and creature. The attitude to creation which has resulted in our current environmental crisis is prayer gone wrong, a lack of poetry. It is idolatry, in the sense of worshipping as absolute what is not God and not recognizing what God has created as gift, but instead subjecting it to the objectifying gaze and control of a neon consciousness. This is both an outer problem – of politics, economics, justice – and an inner problem, a problem of attitude, attention, orientation. I believe it is the combination of both aspects which makes this a spiritual and sacramental issue.

The problem is that we no longer see creation as icon: as an invitation to depth in relationship, to being-with. When creation is reduced to being a thing or commodity we use, buy, sell and destroy, it is no longer a gift to be received with thanks and offered back to its holy source.

The prayer in Duffy's poem comes as a gift and call that

echoes through the trees and trains, the piano scales and names that make up the web of our world. The strange place names from the Shipping Forecast signal an otherness at the edge of our maps of awareness. Prayer is longing and lament, rejoicing and response – but it is always woven into the song of creation itself in its love of otherness.

John Berger's fabulous book *About Looking* details how humans and animals once met across an abyss of mystery and myth.[3] Now, with wilderness domesticated, animals are confined. In zoos, we seek our missing non-human companions, we seek otherness. However, our gaze is one expecting only entertainment, distraction and control. The look of the animal, deprived of its habitat, is unfocused, unworlded. There is no need to romanticize nature, or ignore the real suffering, tragedy and death within it, to realize that something in the Eucharistic song of creation has been interrupted in these wayward stares.

I suggest we should think about the theology of creation, not solely through the overburdened texts of Genesis 1—2, but with the deep and ancient scriptural tradition which sees creation caught up in praise of its source or formed by an intimate relationship with God as giver and feeder. These texts are poetic: they share in the movement of creation itself.

Remember just how much Scripture sings with the poetic word, a word which is an invitation to share the song of creation and the new song of God's grace. A wonderful text for this is Psalm 104, where we can note the sacramental undertones (as in Psalm 23 and many other places): creation is a banquet! Here are verses 10—15:

You make springs gush forth in the valleys;
    they flow between the hills,
giving drink to every wild animal;
    the wild asses quench their thirst.
By the streams the birds of the air have their habitation;
    they sing among the branches.
From your lofty abode you water the mountains;
    the earth is satisfied with the fruit of your work.

---

3 John Berger, *About Looking*, London: Bloomsbury, 2009.

You cause the grass to grow for the cattle,
 and plants for people to use,
to bring forth food from the earth,
 and wine to gladden the human heart,
oil to make the face shine,
 and bread to strengthen the human heart.

Note also, in the psalm, how creation through the Spirit is not
something once-for-all in the past but a continually renewed
activity, grounding the gift and response of creation.

A more explicit evocation of the song of creation is found in
Psalm 148. Here are a few verses (3–4, 7–10):

Praise him, sun and moon;
 praise him, all you shining stars!
Praise him, you highest heavens,
 and you waters above the heavens!

Praise the LORD from the earth,
 you sea monsters and all deeps,
fire and hail, snow and frost,
 stormy wind fulfilling his command!

Mountains and all hills,
 fruit trees and all cedars!
Wild animals and all cattle,
 creeping things and flying birds!

We can find many, many other examples in the psalms and
elsewhere, such as Psalm 96, or the morning stars that sing
for joy in the book of Job. (One such text will be familiar to
those who use the Roman Catholic Divine Office, as it is used
at morning prayer on Sundays and festivals: Daniel 3.57–88, a
great litany of creation's praise to God.[4])

In the New Testament, the key texts are those that hymn
the cosmic scope of God's work in Christ, 'in whom all things

---

4 In Bibles based on the Hebrew text, Daniel chapter 3 ends at verse
30; however, Catholic Bibles include further verses found in Greek
manuscripts.

hold together', a work made possible by the Spirit: Colossians 1, Ephesians 1, John 1, Hebrews 1, Romans 8. Christ is never understood in isolation but as the principle of life, law, light, relatedness and manifestation known in and through creation. They make clear that Christian, incarnate, sacramental theology has never been about rescuing souls one by one from the clutches of an abandoned world.

These texts continually nurture the faith that we are becoming children of God, born of God, through grace, through adoption, through the death and resurrection of Christ; but they do so in this cosmic context, the great liturgy of creation, the gift of the world offered back to God, and Christ present in all his fullness in that offering – as in every Eucharist. It is a deeply Trinitarian vision, in which the Spirit of Christ, the same Spirit of creation, is the one in Hebrews who 'seals us', whose outbreathing by Jesus is the culmination of John, who in Romans intercedes for us with sighs too deep for words. This is no accident; it is the same Spirit who broods over creation, who draws life out of the void, who is within us, who also gives voice to our wordless longing and carries us along in the stream of creation's song of lament and praise. I would say it is not so much that creation is a foreshadowing of the Eucharist but that creation itself is Eucharistic and sacramental in its very being. For us, creation is made known through the lens of *epiclesis*: the Eucharistic moment of the descent of the Spirit 'like dewfall' to transform the elements of our offering.

Creation is thus deeply, eucharistically entwined with the incarnation of the Word and the outpouring of the Spirit – and with justice, the feeding of everyone. Creation is not a mere prelude or stage for the human history of salvation. It is, in its heart, a relationship of offering and response, enfleshment and inspiration. Perhaps this is why the language of poetry and praise is not mere decorative expression of the doctrine of creation but its living and precise truth.

The structure of this collection

I hope the example of how we think of creation helps to unpack a sense of poetry as participation in mystery, in a register that cannot be translated (without loss) into prose. The poetry in this collection is not all explicitly about creation, though I hope readers will spot insistent undercurrents that connect the themes and voices of the verse to that wider context.

As prayer poems, these pieces deliberately sit on the boundary between genres. Some are more obviously devotional, or may more easily be 'adopted' as prayers than others. All of them engage, in one way or another, with the dynamism of Scripture, tradition and experience.

The book has a simple structure. Part 1 contains pieces that I see as a kind of call to prayer, a restless witness to being pulled into something larger. Part 2 comprises material relevant to Advent, Christmas and Epiphany, while Part 3 focuses on Lent, Easter and Pentecost. Part 4 relates to the great expanse of 'ordinary time'; these poems are often related to a specific festival, which is noted unless it is obvious from the title. Finally, Part 5 offers reflections on and with Mary, the mother of God.

How the material is 'used' may, of course, vary. Some may well just want to read in their own way and in their own order. However, the structure facilitates a way of reading that follows the seasons of the Church's year. Individually, this might accompany a period of silence, prayer and reflection at an appropriate time. When used in collective gatherings, care needs to be taken that material taken from books such as these does not displace Scripture. That said, there are often opportunities for readings from non-scriptural sources to be included in informal and formal occasions of worship. As with any reading, I would always suggest that silence surrounds it, to let the words resonate where possible.

Some material is arranged in sequences – for example, the pieces which follow the course of Holy week – and it may make sense to use them in that way, either as daily or weekly food for reflection, or to accompany a structured meditation, such as the stations of the cross.

A recurring sequence in several sections of the book is that of the 'Mysteries'. These are based on the traditional sets of meditations associated with praying the rosary. Unlike the other pieces, these are written in a sonnet form.[5] I realize the rosary itself may be a form of prayer unfamiliar to those who are not in the Roman Catholic or Anglo-Catholic traditions, so a few words of explanation may help.

The rosary is a set of 50 beads on a circular chain or thread. Each set of ten beds (a decade) is divided from the others by a small medallion (which may have a representation of Christ, Mary or a saint on it). In addition, there is a further line of five beads coming off the circle, which ends in a cross.

The rosary can be used as an aid to prayer in many ways, but the most common method follows a pattern. The one praying begins by holding the cross; after an opening response, and sometimes the creed, they move to hold the first bead and say the 'Our Father'. On each of the next three beads, a 'Hail Mary' is said. On the final bead before we get to the big circle, the 'Glory be to the Father' is said. The prayer then moves to the first of the medallions. On each medallion, a 'mystery' is briefly introduced. This will typically be an episode from the life, death and resurrection of Christ. Relevant Scripture is read, and there may be silence and intercession. The 'Our Father' is said. The one praying then passes the rosary through their hands; on each of the ten beads following, a 'Hail Mary' is said, rounded off with a 'Glory be' and sometimes a prayer collect, before moving on to the next medallion, where a new mystery is introduced. In all, five mysteries and sets of beads are prayed. At the end there are closing prayers, and possibly a Marian anthem such as the *Salve Regina*.

For those unfamiliar with it, the rosary may be tainted with the suspicion of being a superstitious or merely mechanical way of praying. However, this is a one-sided view. In fact, the repetitive nature of the rosary draws us into a state of

---

5 There is an obvious comparison with Malcolm Guite's wonderful collection, *Sounding the Seasons: Seventy Sonnets for the Christian Year*, London: Canterbury, 2012; though I can honestly say I had written nearly all of my own sonnets before reading Malcolm's work!

contemplation, where the analysing mind steps aside (as in chanting). Each 'mystery' is exactly that: an unfathomable depth and richness for meditation.

Added to this, the rosary is a supremely tactile form of prayer. It gives the hands something to do, of course, but there is more to it than that: it incarnates prayer, roots us in a simple bodily action. The passing of beads through the hand becomes itself an embodied link to Christ, to the rhythm of prayer in creation, and the handing on of prayer through the centuries.

The sequences of mysteries found in this book are those most central to the Catholic tradition as it has developed. The Joyful Mysteries centre on the birth and childhood of Christ, from the annunciation to the disappearance in the Temple. The Sorrowful Mysteries follow Christ's passion. The Glorious Mysteries focus on the resurrection and its aftermath, including Mary's assumption and coronation. The Luminous Mysteries meditate on key events in the adult Jesus's life and ministry. Aside from these core sequences, many other ways of praying the rosary have been developed over time. One example is The Mysteries of Joseph, also used as the basis for a sequence of poems in this book.

Whether or not you actually use the rosary itself, the mysteries and the pieces based on them can be used in a sequence of prayerful meditations. However, I do encourage anyone who has not done so to use them alongside the physical rosary: it helps to get us out of our heads and into our hands, into the flesh of our praying.

As I have said, the traditional understanding and use of the rosary associates it strongly with the figure of Mary. With that in mind, and also with an eye on Part 5, 'In the School of Mary', I want to end with a few words on why she plays an important role in this collection.

Cultivating the Word: Mary

The figure of Mary, and devotion to her, is a topic which has been a source of division in the Church. In Anglicanism, it can be heard as a partisan Anglo-Catholic marker of identity (though I am quite happy myself to identify as Anglo-Catholic!). That understandings of Mary are divisive should be a cause of sadness for all us, and I'm hopeful that there is now a greater sense of openness to this rich and Christ-centred stream running through the heart of our tradition.

So why do I hold that Mary is important, even crucial, to a fuller immersion in Christian faith? Well, in the creed we declare our belief in the communion of saints. So clearly, core to our faith is our relationship in communion. But God's communion is not limited by the boundaries of our present life, much less our imagination. The saints are those who live in God's presence, who share the eternal song of praise which echoes in creation. For me, it is perfectly natural to turn to the saints, to see them as icons of Christ; as examples, yes; but also as those who share right now in that offering of praise and joy. It's as natural for me to ask for a saint's prayer as it is to ask for a friend's.

In that communion of saints, that offering of praise and joy, Mary takes a special place. It was central to the Church's affirmation of the full divinity of Christ that Mary was given the title *Theotokos* or Mother of God, at councils accepted as authoritative by the mainstream Christian traditions. Simply put, without Mary, no Jesus; incarnation does not happen without Mary's 'yes'. That does not make Mary divine or more important than Jesus, for she is always pointing to Jesus: but she brings Jesus into the world in a way that is unique. Her response to God, her witness of flesh, courage and poetry, speaks to the heart of so many things we have touched on: our praying, solidarity and part in creation's song. If we honour Mary as Mother of God – and so as *our* mother (following Jesus's words from the cross at John 19.27) – we refuse any dualism which pits spirit against creation or spirit against matter.

Mary stands not only for the human response to God but also for the capacity of creation to bear, nurture and manifest the Word of God. She affirms that creation is co-worker with God, not simply a passive instrument. This carries through into all aspects of Mary's presence in the Scriptures. Mary listens, attends, ponders, keeps in her heart, keeps watch by the cross, receives the Spirit at Pentecost; and always, this brings us back to encounter the Word made flesh.

Mary is the first disciple, then, and often seen as a symbol of the Church and of believers. She is also the original Christian contemplative; standing with her, we too can learn to see creation anew, and be drawn to the Word in whom it all belongs together. To be 'in the school of Mary' is to learn to pray with her, in the depths of her connection to the living, embodied mystery of the Word.

Donald Allchin's book on Mary in Anglicanism, *The Joy of All Creation*, is useful here. In his chapter on the seventeenth-century divine, Mark Frank, Allchin notes how Mary is connected with the fruitfulness of creation, the good earth open to God's grace and mercy which shower down from heaven upon it:

> The notion of the human being as a microcosm has a very special relevance here, for Mary may be seen as herself the land of promise, at the heart and centre of creation, as it turns itself towards God . . . [Frank calls her] 'blessed in the fruit of her body, and the blessed child Jesus' but also 'Blessed in the fruit of her ground, her cattle her kine and her sheep, in the inferior of her faculties of her soul and body; all fructify to Christ.'[6]

Allchin connects this with the long Eastern tradition of creation raised up to share in the divine nature, overcoming any split between spirit and flesh. Indeed, he quotes this affirmation of Maximus the Confessor: 'The Word of God, who is God, wills always and in all things to work the mystery of his embodiment.'

Historically, there has been a danger of dualism in the Church's theology, not least where Mary is concerned. I mean that piety which turns Mary into the passive female consort of a hyper-masculine Godhead and seeks to purge her of the 'impurity' of sex, gender, race and embodiment.

---

6 A. M. Allchin, *The Joy of all Creation: An Anglican Meditation on the Place of Mary*, London: New City, 1993, pp. 93–4.

That would see us fall back into the split world view which has become so ecologically destructive, and so damaging to women and our overall understanding of our fleshly life. If Mary is our mother and queen of creation, and mother of the incarnate God, she cannot be a disembodied, unearthly projection of our gender hang-ups. No, Mary points us to Christ, the Word made flesh, whom she bears in her body and in her hands. That body is specific and does not conform to the notion that the white male is the normative human being or believer. And Mary's marginality also sets us free to imagine her in other ways, manifest to many cultures.

This brings us back to our earlier discussion: creation understood in terms of fruitfulness, an incarnate capacity for life, and an offering to God of song, poetry and praise. Mary – this young, Middle Eastern woman with no status or voice in her world – is mother of God, but this also makes her singer, prophet and (I would say) priest, one who in a distinctive way makes the offering of creation.

In this connection, I love the invocation of Mary composed by the medieval mystic Hildegard of Bingen, 'Hail, O greenest branch'. There we see how creation, fruitfulness, manifestation and feasting are joined in a stunning poem of creation:

Hail, o greenest branch
who sprang forth in the airy breeze
of the prayers of the saints.
So the time has come that
you flourished
in your boughs,
hail, hail to you,
because the heat of the sun radiated
in you like the aroma of balm.
For in you bloomed the beautiful
flower which scented all parched
perfumes.
And all things have been manifested
in their full verdure.
Whence the skies set down dew on the
pasture, and all the earth was made

more joyful because her womb produced
grain, and because the birds of Heaven
built their nests in her.
Then the harvest was made ready for
Man, and a great rejoicing of
banqueters, because in you,
o sweet Virgin, no joy is lacking.
All these things Eve rejected.
Now let there be praise to you in the Highest.[7]

We need, then a sacramental and poetic spirituality, one which
is shaped by the Icon of Christ and the song of Mary, which
is mystical, political, embodied and deeply in love with God's
fruitful giving, so much that it wants to give everything as
an offering to God. In such a spirituality, our wastefulness,
cruelty, neglect and exploitation of creation become affronts to
the divine: prayer gone wrong, a lack of poetry.

And for all that we need practical policies and actions to
address issues such as the environmental crisis, we also need a
kind of letting go: a sense of creation as gift, a sense of prayer
as the Spirit's creative breath, in which we rest, and which
bears us like the tide.

I hope, in a small way, this collection may serve that need.

The Feast of Our Lady of Walsingham, 2021

---

7 Cited in Craig Wright, *Listening to Music*, Belmont, CA: Wads-
worth/Thomson Learning, 2000, p. 67.

Acknowledgements

I am very grateful to all who encouraged or inspired me in this project. I'd especially like to thank Sally Bower, Patrice Haynes, Anthia Haynes, Duane Williams, Eleanor Rees, Fr Richard Peers, Christine Smith at Canterbury Press and all my siblings in the Sodality of Mary, Mother of Priests.

PART I

On the Way to Prayer

Lost

Click.
The email was sent;
dry earth,
rattling on the wood.

I sat back,
tried to correct my hunched shoulders.
Evening slouched through the room.

A nameless bird sang
outside the window.
The wine glass
reached for me.

Was I completely lost
or simply waiting
to be
found?

Divine Office

Seven times a day I praise you (Ps. 119.164)

I saw seven lights
and in the midst
a human one
shining like the sun

I took seven breaths
and in the pause
a pulse of grace
wilder than the wind

I held seven thorns
and on my palm
a wounded prayer
crying like a child

I loved seven stars
and in the sky
a word of longing
deeper than the dark

I said seven prayers
and on my lips
a taste of God
sweeter than the night

Praying with Grass

A dialogue with Scriptures (Deut. 32.2; 2 Sam. 23.4; Ps. 72.6; Ps. 103.15; Isa. 40.6; Isa. 66.14; Matt. 6.29–30; John 6.10)

'All flesh is grass':
in this word
all we are
is given to death,
our sister death.

I have felt grass,
seen it dance,
caught its scent,
brushed its yielding stems.
It has blessed me.

Read with new eyes:
grass is grace,
kissed by rain,
catching summer light.
It holds the earth.

To ruined streets
and dry dust
grass brings life,
clothed in king's glory.
It is newness.

A place to sit
to break bread
and touch hands
on the open ground.
It has no fear.

The Word made flesh:
made garden,
made dewfall;
'your bones shall flourish
like the green grass'.

Falling

I am so tired
of grasping all that cannot be owned
the density of death
I want so much
to let go
to fall

to fall
to let go
I want so much
the gravity of grace
of loving all that cannot be owned
I am so touched

into the swallow's nest
into the heart's wide acres
I fall
to you
in love
in love
with you
I fall

PART 2

Advent, Christmas and Epiphany

Strange Genealogies: Matriarchs, Prophets and Mothers

An alternative Advent Sequence

I. Sarah

I also walked
away from known stories,
away from the world formed
by familiar tongues.

I also bore
the burden of God's dreams.
I stood at the tent door
and laughed in disbelief.

But I alone
was used by my husband;
passed off as his sister,
my body his defence.

Do you judge me?
When Hagar and her child
were forced into the wastes,
I held my son tight.

Do you wonder
what I did, what I said
when my son was brought home,
rope burns on his young wrists?

Do you know me?
Know what it is to live
without security
at the frayed canvas edge?

One day I'll go
from the oak-shadowed tent;
I'll welcome God's angels
and sit to eat with them.

I will turn and
find my sister Hagar
passing the broken bread,
forgiveness in her eyes.

II. Tamar

I was widow weave, cut from the loom,
thrown away with the scraps,
waiting on the will of men.

Now I sit by the side of the road to Timnah.
I shed my mourning skin
and wait in my own way.

Call me whore, call me sex worker,
call me black widow:
I choose my own margin.

I am risk-bearer, pledge-taker,
taking what power I can
when no choice is easy.

I will survive, make my own place,
raise my own child,
take back my own name.

So I sit by the side of the road to Timnah,
holding the scarlet thread
that leads to Bethlehem.

III. Rahab

I know you saw me
before you looked away.
I was there: hidden in plain view
living in the walls of your soul
under the sign of shame.

It did not stop you
from eyeing me slantwise,
approaching me on unseen paths
paying the fee for possession
under a crimson lamp.

You did not suspect
I opened other doors,
hid promises beneath the flax
fibres of your traitor heart,
let them go in secret.

I was your shadow,
with unsuspected life
teeming beneath my scarlet wings –
keening to wheel and sing with joy
when the dams broke and fell.

I am mother, whore,
host. I wait to welcome
the child to whom the door is closed.

IV. Ruth

I am un-relation
un-kin.
My name is foreign.

I am told to go
back where I came from.
I rely on the kindness
of those who have power.
I am bargained over
like a bushel of wheat or a wash bowl.

But I do not want your pity:
I stay, I make my own bed.
I walk the miles worn by devotion,
work the fields sown by strangers.
My blood is not yours
but it runs from an undivided heart;
it crosses bloodlines and boundaries
to break on the shore of a strange saviour.

I am fore-mother,
queer kin.
My name is: friend.

V. Bathsheba

Look at me.
Look without seeing.
Read the straight lines
that record just
his murderous gaze,
his taking.

Am I there,
on the bright rooftop?
Have I gone down
to the lost world,
the shining white space
of the text?

All those eyes,
all those painter's tricks
to lay me bare
in the half light
of a fantasy,
a cliché.

Do you hear?
Do I cry at night
hidden from view?
Does it echo,
my voice, my lost choice,
my bleeding?

I will rise.
I will leave that house,
walk through the crowd
unseen, unknown,
touch a trailing hem
take my gift.

He will ask
'Who took my power?'
I will face him
and say my name
from the secret ark
of my strength.

VI. Mary's sisters

I am Miriam
alive between the walls of the deep
singing the mighty into the mud

I am Deborah
commander, judge and mother of Israel
holding court in the green palm shade

I am Hannah
celebrant of divine reversals
cutting the cord of fate with prayer

I am Abigail
descended from the mountain heights
stilling the bloodlust of kings

I am Huldah
keeper of the dark speech of God
prophesying pain and penitence

I am Esther
veiled queen of the resistance
foiling the hand of genocide

I am Eve
mother of all the living
tending my shadowed garden

I am Mary
mother of God
mother of faith
Christ-bearer
star of the deeps below
and the night above:
prophet, singer, witness, priest

one of many sisters

The Joyful Mysteries

I. The Annunciation

When Mary found the angel at her door,
she gave no thought to flight or flaming wing.
Though sense and sight were shaken to their core,
in wonder deep her soul began to sing.
Hers the Amen that sets creation free;
no man will speak for her or bind her heart.
She is the earth renewed, the shining sea,
the compass rose that rights our wayward chart.
With her the poor and shamed are raised above,
their broken bodies hallowed and restored.
Her faith and flesh will feed the Word of love;
within her womb, the One the stars adored.
   The angel left, his heart disarmed to see
   that God must wait her mortal 'Let it be'.

II. The Visitation

All joy is gift, a call from deep to deep;
it takes the road and does not hide its face.
So Mary ran alone her joy to reap,
her heart a wild and open sky of grace.
What promise drew her on, what shadow sight?
What word of blessing calling to be born?
Two women met in ordinary light,
through touch and smile they hailed the coming dawn.
As empires built their hills of skull and bone,
Elizabeth felt hope leap up within.
She hailed a hidden king, a humbler throne,
a new creation yearning to begin.
    And Mary sings a world turned upside down,
    a day when One who serves will wear the crown.

III. The Birth of Jesus

Who can divine the deeps and flows of birth?
Not the cold world, that walks with heavy tread
to bar its doors against those of no worth;
that tends its fear and lies down with the dead.
Outside its hostile walls, a woman cried
in pain and joy to wake the midnight sun.
With all her strength, she crossed the deep divide
and through her flesh the birth of love was won.
What night is this, so wonderful and strange
that animal and angel join in awe?
A miracle of hope, a breath of change,
and in the wall of death – an open door.
  Upon the child's face her tired eyes shine,
  and welcome to life a weakness divine.

IV. The Presentation of Jesus at the Temple

Let us go to the altar of delight,
where the sparrow nests in Wisdom's embrace,
where Simeon treads the threshold of night,
awaits the shining presence of God's face.
Mary comes forward as prophet and priest,
the body of love held out in her hands.
It is the birthing of the promised feast;
the sea of years will break upon the sands
of hope and exile, singing and lament.
The aged eye of Simeon sees true
that love's insistence never will relent
until the aching world has been made new.
  The joy that Mary tastes is laced with loss,
  her soul the harbour of a shadowed cross.

V. The Disappearance and Finding of Jesus at the Temple

Nothing and no one, a fugitive child
alone in the halls of sacred glory;
no right to be there, a boy running wild,
tracing the line of a turning story.
He comes to test the wise, to scale the wall,
to overturn the tables of learning,
to follow the freedom of Wisdom's call
and kindle the flame of human yearning.
He is found in the heart of God's own seat,
whose stones cry out in praise and sacrifice.
His blood is wine, his hands the ripened wheat,
his heart of love will pay the promised price.
    Into the depths of Mary's heart there fell
    a nameless treasure more than words could tell.

The Mysteries of Joseph

I. Joseph descended from David

When the soil was bare and barren
and the hard ground unforgiving,
the root drank deep and dreamed of light.
Hidden, silent, ceaselessly wending
to silver dew and morning sun,
the root made its persistent path.

Joseph was the child of the root,
heir of fallen kings, wayward sons
and foreign women who refused
to hide their faith or lose their name.
He took the tangled growth of time
and cleared a way for hope to bloom.

II. Joseph the Just Man

It would have been easy
to pick up the stone,
to feel its weight,
to let it fly.

Joseph did not condemn
or follow the script
of wounded pride
and shaming lie.

He was just to his love,
who one day would sing
of fallen thrones,
the poor raised high.

III. Joseph following a Dream takes Mary as his Wife

Joseph gave himself to sleep,
gave himself to angel-sight.
The veil of this world was rent
and God whispered in the night.

He dreamed of the Spirit's shade,
of his Mary's hidden life.
He looked at her with new eyes,
blessed that she would be his wife.

IV. Joseph warned in a Dream takes Mary and Jesus into Egypt

Wherever exiles flee in fear,
with men of violence at their heels
and only uncertainty ahead:
look to the side of the road.

There, walking with them, you may see
a man driven by dreams and hope,
holding the hand of his pregnant wife,
sheltering his displaced God.

V. Joseph the Carpenter

He feels close to God
in this work of making,
of crafting true
the mortise and tenon of the world.

He makes things of use,
carves stone of home and hearth.
His hands think deep,
follow the hidden grain of the world.

Beside him, a child
gathers fallen pieces,
holds in his palm
broken fragments of an untold world.

Joseph works and dreams
of roots that lie hidden,
ready to grow
into trees of healing for the world.

For the Winter Solstice

Speak to us, child of winter hope,
womb-dark in your promise.
Lie with us in the night of earth
tomb-black in your coming.

This night so full of letting go,
the serpent sheds its skin.
And death extends a raven wing
to guard the new-born light.

The Angel's View

I walk the winds
placeless, pure intellect.
I sing harmony
with my sweet angelkind.

I could have stayed
whole in the undimmed light
hiding my dark fear
that one day I would fall.

But he called me
to take the downward stair
to take the strange weight
of the earth beneath me.

I spoke to her:
she was young, unafraid.
She took my words, weighed them;
her 'yes' sent me soaring.

Now I watch them
from the edge of sky,
while my kin sing glory
over the house of beasts.

And I feel it,
impossible to miss:
gravity's sharp pull,
the mass of grace made flesh.

The air is cold;
ice crystals on the wing
crackle as I unfurl,
breathe, and fall into joy.

Magus

Follow the thread of asters
drifting across the night field;
a dusting of divine tears
to light the barren hollows.

Take a flower from the stem
(he loves me, he loves me not)
tell of a father's grief
(he loves me, he loves me not).

Walk on; the scentless flower
will spiral into incense,
gleam gold on your trembling palm,
anoint your dying old soul.

Take the path of alchemy
and come to the manger side;
give your flower to the hand
of the love you had misplaced.

Return by another way.

PART 3

Lent, Easter and Pentecost

Ashes to Ashes

We're burning the world to ash
to the fag-end of fossil fuel
scorching the skies above
turning the living soil to sand.

We're using it all up now
wearing, tearing it all out
buying, selling, owning
and sending it all to hell.

This is no volcano promising rebirth
no earth rising phoenix-like
from the blackened ground
of fertility and flaming hope.

We have to turn around now
back to the gift of creation
back to the song of the living
shining with the Spirit's dew.

So take the ash upon your head
know you are a passing guest
feel the fragility of living things
the desert spaces in our soul.

Follow one in whose steps
the desert blooms and riots
the one whose cross is rooted
in the suffering of the earth.

Deserter

Leave the path behind
and with it, the world.
Walk on rocks dismayed to dust
by sun, wind and time.
Go where the air covers your traces:
sand silting down like cinders,
like memories lost to fire.

Tread light to your name
and to your bloodlines.
Walk into the otherworld;
let it unshape you.
Go to the limit of what can be
known, or said, or sensed. Be still
in the eye of the darkness.

Is this a severance,
an escape from life?
You will walk with blind angels,
sit with those who are not
human, whose stories are secret lairs,
who bear the song of their blood
under feather, scale and fur.

One day you'll come back
across the dead sea.
Your eyes will shine with strangeness,
the light of a wild star.
In your palm will be a desert rose,
a gift from the other side,
from silence, and the world's end.

The Sorrowful Mysteries

I. The Agony in the Garden

The sleepless trees held vigil as he prayed
and friends fell fast into the arms of sleep.
In agony of faith, his heart dismayed,
he stood apart and called from deep to deep.
Did he recall a garden, long since lost,
where hands reached out to grasp the bitter fruit?
Did drops of bloody sweat betray the cost
that would be paid to water love's new shoot?
When we wrestle demons through the night
as pale fear wears the grinning mask of death,
he shares our darkened path, our lonely fight,
the broken prayers we speak under our breath.
    Then: shouting, orders, a drawing sword's hiss;
    a loved one, arms open, waiting a kiss.

II. The Scourging at the Pillar

The barbed tongues write their script of pain and blood,
inscribe the claim of those who hold the whip:
'We are the ones whose force defines the good;
and through our touch of power we will rip
your skin from bone till all that shows is shame.'
Healing hands restrained, voice of peace denied,
he bore upon his back the curse and blame,
stood firm with all whose blood for judgement cried.
There was no place too low for Christ to reign,
no torture that could make God's grace retreat.
In bitter depths of cruelty's domain,
still the incarnate heart of love will beat.
    In hidden rooms, where hope curls up to die,
    there Christ comes in to raise the victim high.

III. The Crowning with Thorns

'Sit here, your majesty, while we prepare
your splintered throne, your high and mighty seat!
We'll lend you choicest purple robes to wear
and take those pauper's sandals from your feet.
We'll give you gifts, the chief of which is pain,
and praise you as a king and living god.
A crown will show what fills your kingly vein;
your trembling hands will hold the bloodied rod.'
He took what they offered, carried the thorn
that choked the life buried within them still.
He took the fear they hid behind their scorn,
kept in his heart the love they could not kill.
    A king, a slave, our God, our poverty;
    our victim and the one to set us free.

IV. The Carrying of the Cross

Feel the sheer weight of it: the fallen tree
bearing down from lost forests, deadened heart
within its splintered skin, washed-up debris
of Eden's rent and ruined work of art.
Those who rule the earth now carve the cold wood
and shape it to a sign of shame and death;
cruel parody of life, watered with blood,
promising only a last tortured breath.
He lifts it up, the rubbish of the world,
walks the long way of oppression and tears.
His torn back bent like a dying leaf curled,
he falls, he falls to the echo of jeers.
    Unknown, the love that has begun to reign;
    unseen, the rose that grows against the grain.

V. The Crucifixion

What is the cross? The tree of life lost, life
gained; the frame of a door, swinging open
to the farther shore; a wood-handled knife
for paring the soul, the heart that's broken;
a hammer for idols, the fruitful vine
promising new wine for the dispossessed;
sheltering branches for kith and for kine,
an altar where bread is broken and blessed:
blessed in the shade of the hungering dark,
for the cross takes root under a veiled sun,
where a nailed Son redeems heartwood and bark,
carved on his workbench, till love's work is done.
    He hangs there: victim, priest, cursed slave and king,
    the first healing leaf of a verdant spring.

tree of life

climb the hill with me
against the tide of footprints
leading away from
the summit

walk up to the tree
that holds the sky
branches paralysed
in prayer

let senses bend the knee
to this counterpoint
of wood and nail and
flesh

touch the wound where he
becomes river and flood
heart opened wide
to you

look and learn to see
in the absence of sun
what cannot be shown by any
other light

Wings of Wounded Glory

*A sequence of prayer poems for Holy Week and Easter
based on the Gospel reading set for the daily Eucharist
or other principal service.*

Monday in Holy Week: John 12.1–11

God of overflowing life:
through the way of Jesus Christ your Son,
you draw us into the depths of your passion.

He came to his friends,
to Mary, Martha and Lazarus,
sharing their table,
unbinding their hearts and minds.

As Mary poured out her gift,
so Christ empties himself for love.

As Mary filled the house with fragrance,
so Christ lavishes grace without measure.

As Mary broke the jar to offer what she had,
so Christ breaks his heart and his tomb
for the world he came to save.

May we know and cherish the touch and sight and scent
of this love made flesh,
this mystery of body and blood,
which is the gift of Jesus Christ,
the perfect offering.

We ask this in his name,
in his heart.

Tuesday in Holy Week: John 12.20–36

He rises, he rises:
lifted above the world
by cruelty and shame.

Held in place by hatred,
wings pinioned
by an empire's fear.

He falls, he falls:
into the welcoming earth,
into darkness and silence.

From the deeps he harrows,
splitting the seed,
disputing with death.

And he will rise again
on wings of wounded glory.
And we will rise with him,
holding the grain in our hands.

Wednesday in Holy Week: John 13.21–32

Christ our undying star
we offer you the lightless places of our lives.

In poverty and exile
Mary gave birth to you;
and it was night

In fear and longing
Nicodemus searched for you;
and it was night

In weakness and zeal
Judas betrayed you;
and it was night

Come to us
in the pain of birth
and the fear of falling

Come to us
in the pathless dark
and the shadow of seeking

Come to us
in the cold of loss
and the time of crisis

Bring us to your table laid
and feed us with yourself;
find in us the ember light
and breathe it into fire.

For the darkness is not dark to you.
For the night and the day are yours
– as are we.

Maundy Thursday: John 13.1–17, 31–35

'You do not know now what I am doing.'

We did not know:
when you took off the robe of power
and knelt before the water.

We did not know:
when your love took away from us
the dirt of the weary road.

But now we can see:
in the work of carers and nurses
in hospitals and homes.

Every dressing changed, every bedpan emptied,
every breath eased, every foot washed:
a sacrament of care.

Teach us the new commandment:
a revolution of love
beyond shame and honour,
beyond power and control.

Teach us the authority of service given,
community created,
hope renewed
in the shadow of death and fear.

'You do not know now what I am doing
but later you will understand.'

Good Friday: John 18 and 19

Jesus Christ, liberate us
from a world that crucifies
those who challenge it.

The world has many questions:
Where are you from?
What have you done?
What is your status?
What is your truth?

And you reply:
I am not from here.
I am he.
I am . . .
a victor without a victim
a king without a kingdom
a truth in flesh and blood
a life undefined by death.

With Mary your Mother
and John your Beloved,
with the refugee, the undocumented,
the homeless and the poor,
let us be a new community:
a communion of saints without borders,
formed by the grace that flows from the cross.

Jesus Christ, liberate us
for a new creation
budding from the twisted tree.

Holy Saturday: John 19.38–end/Matthew 27.57–end

I pray to an absent God.

Why did you call us
with talk of seeds and sparrows
and promises of kingdom come?

Now we see only
trampled dirt around an empty cross,
a tomb sealed and soldiered.
The cup we shared
has turned to bitter wine in our mouth.

Why did you teach
that if we asked for good things
no loving Father would give us a scorpion?

Well, we asked
and the answer has come
with a scorpion sting:
that death is the end
that empires win
that nothing changes.

Why did you leave us?
Why did you fail?
Why don't you just
go to hell?

From his tomb
a lingering scent of spice
and a small insistent pull,
as if to a deeper silence.

I pray to an absent God.

Easter Sunday: John 20.1–18

Christ our Morning Star:
as Mary your Mother
bears the Word of incarnate love
so Mary your Apostle
bears the Word of risen hope.

May she teach us to trust . . .

. . . trust in the not knowing
when feet drag towards the tomb
and it is still dark.

. . . trust in the undoing
when we find ourselves unravelled
and we do not understand.

. . . trust in the weeping
when it is all too much
and tears cannot be contained.

. . . trust in the meeting
when we struggle to find words
and love speaks our name.

. . . trust in the telling
when we are called to witness
and hope lives on through us.

. . . trust in the dying
when through the darkest hour
we step into the dawn.

Unused

They gave him myrrh
mixed with wine
a gift
to ease his pain.

It went unused.

They brought him myrrh
mixed with aloes
a gift
to salve his corpse.

It went unused.

There was no shield
from pain
from death
for him

who rose
like incense
like the fragrance
of an unexpected dawn.

Descended into Hell

Someone lies in a room
alone
waiting
the letter in her hand
trembles

Someone sits in a car
alone
waiting
the knuckles on the wheel
whiten

Someone kneels in a ditch
alone
waiting
the fingers on the gun
aching

Someone leans on a plough
alone
sweating
the hands on the wood
bleeding

The blade works deep
against the grain of the earth
turning over the silence
making space in the darkness
for the seed
alone
waiting

Ecce Homo

Suspended
from the gift of life
to the life of gift
the Human One
breathes his last
expires our shrunken heart

Completed
from the lost garden
to the garden grave
the Dead Christ
opens the womb
harrows our barren earth

Risen
from the formless void
to the empty tomb
the New Adam
fully alive
transforms our longing flesh

Suspended
Completed
Risen
in him who dies for us
in her who bears us:
ecce homo

After the Earthquake

After the earthquake
we went out into the bruised air
not knowing if or how
we might trust the ground
or walk its broken skin.

We followed the fault
of heaven's holy dissonance,
friction of earth and hope;
grave landmarks shifted,
borders were rearranged.

He greeted us there,
dancing with the rising dust,
lit by the lightning's arc,
composing our fear
to a tremor of trust.

After the earthquake
we breathed a different dawn
unknowing, unconfined –
the world recomposed
by the shock of his love.

The Glorious Mysteries

I. The Resurrection

In the silence of death we lost the word
and dark-shuttered days filled with empty sighs;
while, out of our sight, the walls of hell stirred
and long-abandoned eyes began to rise.
Night voices spoke no more of hope stillborn
as women heard the nightjar's lifting song.
They walked the path unfolding in the dawn,
retracing endless years of hurt and wrong,
to One who shone with life no force could hold,
no crushing rock, no steel-armed guard could keep;
his open arms embracing hearts grown cold,
his wounded hands reviving them from sleep.
    He shakes the bone-dead march of history
    and, calling us by name, says 'Rise with me'.

II. The Ascension of Christ into Heaven

Suddenly he is gone; their restless stare
scans the torn clouds and finds only absence;
startled hands rise to hold the empty air,
trying to mould his leaving into sense.
'Why stand and watch?' the angel voices call;
'Why make mystery subject to your gaze?
No one owns him, he is God's all in all;
no power or name on earth will own his ways.
Give up your fear, your urge to fence him in,
to shutter and contain his rainbow lights;
feel now the Spirit's breath upon your skin,
your human nature welcomed in the heights.
    Now go, break bread and make creation new;
    and Christ will come each moment love breaks through.'

III. The Descent of the Holy Spirit

She breathes and beckons formless earth to be;
she broods and beauty grows beneath her wings.
To those weighed down by fear and slavery
she gifts a heart that braves, a soul that sings.
She is the change that settles soft as dew,
and Holy Spirit, wild as wind and flame;
lion-strong and silver-tongued, she speaks anew
the Word made flesh who from the Father came.
She is the Gift, unowned yet pledged to all:
the common wealth that knows not yours and mine,
the seal and strength to break the hateful wall,
the power to make our weakness all divine.
    And when in doubt and fear they try to pray,
      she gives them tongues of fire to wake the day.

IV. The Assumption

This woman's hands: an altar held and kissed
by one whose advent cut the veil of night.
This woman's hair: caught up in his small fist
who clung to her and not to heaven's might.
This woman's song will joyfully subvert
the gilded lie that gives itself a throne.
This woman's eyes will see the hate and hurt,
stare down the hand that casts the judgement stone.
This woman's feet must walk the way of loss,
the beaten roads that take her son away.
This woman's heart must break upon the cross
and soar again to greet the rising day.
    And when death seeks to claim her flesh and soul,
    Love will win her all, Love will keep her whole.

V. The Coronation of Our Lady in Heaven and the Glory of the Saints

I saw her at the demonstration's head,
lifting her friends who had been trodden down;
beneath her woven hair, its greying thread,
there shone the faintest glimmer of a crown.
I saw her walk unbowed through storm and flame,
creating sanctuaries from her song;
and ever on her lips, a whispered name:
a cursed and banished love made heaven-strong.
Round her, the dry stones find their voice of praise,
and wholly human saints, by grace made free,
lend us their prayers to lift our sunken days:
one Body joined in God's own symphony.
    The sun her robe, the moon her shining way,
    she leads us to the heart of Christ the Day.

Come, Holy Gift

What kind of gift is this?
Who can hold the wild wind
running through the fingers,
shivering the water's skin?

She is the womb of the dawn,
the arc of the arrow's flight.
She is perfect stillness, ever moving,
the wing that holds the sky.

She is there when the Word takes flesh,
when he rises from the water.
She is the one who remembers,
the revealer of things to come.

She is the unspoken prayer
when words fumble and fail.
She is fire and fierce defender,
song of the one in the many.

What kind of gift is this:
leading us to the desert,
falling like flame on the altar
caught in the sails of prayer?

Beltane Spirit

Fire
Fire in the heart
of the dark earth
Fire in the distant winter stars
Fire in the soul wide open
to the falling flame of spirit
on the brushwood
of the heart's
fire

PART 4

Transforming Ordinary Time

Ordinary Time

Come down from the mountain.
Did we dream there?
Do shreds of a vision
cling to us still,
petals that dance in the
      thorns?

The days drift and spiral,
going nowhere.
The pain that never left
pulls out a chair.
We have all the time we
      need.

Time stretches and dissolves
too full, too fast.
It is taken from us,
surplus value,
pulse turned to profit and
      loss.

Can we receive again
the gift of time?
Hold the chalice to catch
days distilled in
drops of bloody sweat and
      grace?

And the Word was made time:
one who blesses
nameless miracles of
ordinary love.
Praise the God of unmarked
      hours.

In among the greening,
wildflowers rise.

The Luminous Mysteries

I. The Baptism of Jesus in the Jordan

The river runs from the womb of the dawn,
carries deep down the undertow of grace.
He is drawn to its call, the song reborn,
waters renewed in the light of God's face.
The Baptist lifts a voice of sand and sky,
levels his path to the edge of the known.
The Son of Adam hears the prophet's cry,
remembers that love is not said, but shown.
He is humbled to death beneath the wave,
he thrills with life as he rises once more.
The feathered Spirit signs his power to save,
to turn love's tide to this, our nearer shore.
    A voice of many waters washed the earth
    and blessed the bringer of our second birth.

II. The Wedding at Cana

This ordinary beauty touches deep:
two solitudes fall into sounding rhyme.
Each hidden heart affirms that it will keep
its loving vigil through the tread of time.
Christ comes as guest to share the wedding day;
he spins the warp and weft of love made whole.
Mary brings him the needs of those who pray,
the wine-dark longing of the human soul.
'Do as he says,' she tells the ones who wait,
as Christ imparts the sacramental sign.
This ordinary water bears the weight
of glory, ripe and heavy on the vine.
    They drank to life and joy, to love unknown,
    the secret heart of him who left the throne.

III. The Proclamation of the Kingdom

A voice speaks from the edges of the world,
raises a cry against time's dull despair:
let the path turn, let the heart rise, unfurled
from inward-curving pride and fearful care;
let walls tremble and empires turn to dust
to make way for the servant reign of Christ;
let all our bitter idols fall to rust,
love no more to dumb power sacrificed.
Turn to the light again, you longing heart,
be soil to the poor seed of love's unrest;
and north, south, east and west shall play their part,
with boundless grace to greet the unknown guest.
    In unseen acts of love it will take flight
    and stretch its wings into the circling night.

IV. The Transfiguration

We build dark walls to hide creation's light,
settle for second-hand shades of glory.
He calls us away, draws us to the height,
brings kindling for a different story.
He shows the sun's heart, the bright shining air,
the diamond sparkling of the dancing sea;
he shows us the way to walk with him there,
in uncreated rays of ecstasy.
And when the glow fades and words lose their hold,
he is still the fire from whom we once came;
burning with love in a world grown too cold,
anointing us with a Spirit of flame.
    This is the light that will never grow pale,
    the undying star that never can fail.

V. The Institution of the Eucharist

Under the stare of thirty silver stars,
whose cold gleam longs for colder certainty,
a cup is filled with healing for our scars
and bread is torn to sate our deepest need.
The mystery of blood, the body's grace,
deeper than words can tell or thought can sound:
they call us through the veil of time and space
to touch the heart of him, the king uncrowned.
A table shared with food that has no price,
a feast for all to share the life divine;
the endless dance, the taste of paradise,
Christ present as he is in bread and wine.
    He leaves us no dead coin, no lost recall:
    he lives our life, the All within the all.

Diakonos

It was, otherwise,
such a good, practical idea:
'Let's choose seven:
to wait on tables,
to free up some diary space,
for preaching and for prayer
(and those times we find ourselves in jail).'
So the apostles said
and so they did.

The mistake they made
was the laying on of hands.

You see, the seven followed
a wild, brave, unruly spirit.
They found themselves
preaching to lynch mobs,
baptizing Ethiopian nobility.
Did Stephen and Philip forget?
Did they leave the apostles
with dishes to clean
and tables to wipe?

Or does God work through
the best-laid plans gone awry?

Deacons are ordained to serve
wherever God's table
is laid in the world:
where love puts its body on the line,
forgiveness faces down hate,
grace knows no limit or lack;
and where the one who serves you
has the face of an angel
and the heart of Christ.

The River

Trinity Sunday

Sit by the spring.
It is quiet here,
where hidden waters
hold out their darkness
to kiss the sun.

Test the water.
Taste the earth's depths,
its mineral tang,
a lingering touch
of beginnings.

Walk the river.
Follow its course
down to the valley,
emptying its heart
to the dry plains.

Hear the music,
the flowing word,
wordlessly calling;
see the wild things come
to drink their fill.

Meet the ocean.
Know the moon's pull
to unseen currents
and untrod shorelines.
Take off your shoes.

Feel the wild waves
rob you of weight.
The sea is power
and yielding patience.
It will guide you.

Take the tern's wings
and look down on
font, flow and ocean;
none the other,
none alone.

Watch their circle,
the loving dance
that holds and sets free,
makes space for you
to join the flow.

Hoc est enim corpus meum

Corpus Christi day (Thursday after Trinity Sunday)

I saw the dew settle on his skin
as night fell to darker dawn.
Flesh was weak then;
words weaker still.

Hours before, his hands breaking,
breaking the offered bread,
he gave himself,
kept nothing back.

He would not stay in the past,
reduced to weightless memory,
a cup lifted
to absent friends.

No: he confounds all distance,
defies the ebb of time,
gathers the grain,
pours the new wine.

So urgent, yet so still:
the touch, the nearness of love,
the bitter cross,
sweetness of grace.

Here and now, as then,
he reaches to us from the dark:
'Kiss me, my betrayer, my love:
this is my body.'

Sacred Heart

Friday after the second Sunday after Pentecost

When my heart took flight
I saw it break and die,
a small feathered thing
in the hands of the sky.

When my heart gave out
I felt it sink in me,
a vessel of stone
in the dark of the sea.

My love's heart flowed free
from his wounded side,
an ocean of light
that caught me in its tide.

I would find my heart
made whole in his embrace,
carried to shore on
the breaking wave of grace.

Transfiguration

Looking out from the border of Somerset towards Dorset,
Feast of the Transfiguration 2020

We emerged from the deep green path.
The land fell away from the edge
to fields and unassuming hills.
The A303 breathed and sighed,
troubled and unheeding
of the grey mottled sky.

Something shifted then and shivered,
a boundary was gently crossed.
The clouds did not part or thunder;
they silvered, lit up from within;
and we walked on the arc
of uncreated light.

Another hill, another time,
which is then, and now and always,
the sacred veil is rent in two.
The earth remembers its glory
and one shares his fullness
without measure or price.

They call it miracle and sign,
a wonder that falls from above.
How many ways we have to miss
the heaven we are made to be,
the light that is preserved
in the green of the leaf.

Let names and cages fall away,
the dull divide of mine and yours.
Mystery is the air we breathe,
the grace that lifts the hawk at dawn;
creation and its God,
shining with the same light.

'Today
you will be with me
in paradise'.

Four Quarters

Michaelmas

'at my right hand Michael, at my left hand Gabriel, before me Uriel, behind me Raphael, and above my head, the Presence of God' (from a traditional Jewish bedtime prayer).

Raphael

To the east I turn
and call upon the angel of the dawn
where hawk wings hold the rising air;
across the threshold of the day's beginning
stir the waters of our awakening,
guide us to inner sight.

Michael

To the south I turn
and call upon the angel of the midday sun
fierce in the heat of the chase;
across the threshold of the day's peak
summon our warrior hearts
to fight for nameless loves.

Gabriel

To the west I turn
and call upon the angel of the evening light
sliding into shadowed waters;
across the threshold of the day's declining
pull deep our dream of wisdom
to welcome the coming Christ.

Uriel

To the north I turn
and call upon the angel of the night sky
stretching sable arms between the stars;
across the threshold of the day's ending
carry us from the place of fear
to rest on the dark earth.

Shekinah

I raise my hands above
and call upon the Intimate Presence
as she descends to dwell with us;
across all thresholds of life and death
crown our longing hearts
with divinity.

How to Eat Bread

Sunday of the Word of God in January/
Bible Sunday in October

(with apologies to Miranda Threlfall-Holmes, *How to Eat Bread: 21 Nourishing Ways to Read the Bible*, London: Hodder & Stoughton, 2021)

They told me to eat my bread
sliced, wrapped and white;
preserved against change and decay,
not a crumb out of place.

I took what they gave without question.
It filled me up, that stuff;
it left no space inside for hunger;
on my lips, no taste for wonder.

It began to stick in my throat.
It was all squares and surfaces;
nothing in it remembered
the mystery of the sprouting seed.

Then I found him; selling loaves
in the corner of the market
(though no money changed hands),
his table golden with gifts.

He raised his hands, broke the loaf,
opened to us the memory of fire,
the sour fragrance of yeast,
the breath within the bread.

Now we eat the food of life:
savour the texture of its slow rise,
sense the gathering of its grains,
brush against its hidden heart.

We taste the text of earth and rain;
hands touch the bowing stalks
as we walk the singing fields,
and trust to paths that are not straight.

All Saints

So much unseen –

    a boy comes home
    unlocks the door
    takes the lit cigarette
    from his sleeping father's hand

All those great
distant heroic saints
also had to walk
the familiar earth

    a man reaches out
    touches the hand
    that lies trembling
    on the hospital bed

Now we see them
a long way off
like summer lightning
on distant hills

    a teacher waits
    talks to the girl
    who sits alone
    at the back of her class

But light travels fast
and filaments of faith
of prayer and love
conduct through air and time

      someone speaks out
      a word of hope
      a word that splits
      what's said and done

A strange family
a queer communion
one body alive
in Christ our Life

      – so much alive

All Souls

You can keep your 'next room'
and your 'not really dead'.
Please take your 'passed away',
the poems that you read.

Don't ask me not to cry
or remove the blunt blade
that saws right through my ribs
to the space where I prayed.

Please do not wish on me
your angels, harps and light.
I'll send the bloody lot
to the far side of night.

I'll grieve until I'm numb
for death is truly death.
I'll stare into the void
unsure of my next breath.

See, every crawling hour
will bear death's shadow mark
until prayer lifts its head,
speechless in the dark.

Love cannot live with lies
but live, and live it will
on roads of blood and bone
beneath the cross-backed hill.

I'll sing with all the souls,
we'll grieve and we'll grieve well.
I'll see no Easter day
till I have walked in hell.

The stubbornness of grief
is my mass for the dead.
Simple food, peace, tales told
and wine the deepest red.

PART 5

In the School of Mary

Mary's Hands

Her hands are still now,
crossed like sparrow wings
fallen from a storm-washed sky.
In the cup of her palm
a promise hides,
a feather made of glass.
She lets it sing.

She holds the rein tight,
holds the path ahead
to Spirit knows where or when.
She feels the future kick,
her body stretched,
liminal and tired.
She works the weave.

She cradles her child
as he bawls and feeds
under cold and outcast stars.
She cleans the sick and shit,
wonders how God
can be this needy flesh.
She raises him.

Her hands make a shield
from the swords of men,
from the gaze that seeks her shame.
She is tabernacle,
a hunted ark
upon the exile sea.
She finds a way.

She bears her burden
across the threshold
to the house of blood and ash.
She feels the old ones' songs,
her heart reshaped
to take the absent weight.
She offers him.

She traces the hollow,
interrupts the meal:
'Do what he tells you,' she says.
She makes room for wonder;
water is poured,
the vessels brim with change.
She lifts the wine.

See tears in her hands
and blood in the earth,
a splinter lodged in her nail.
She fashions an altar,
crosses the lines,
the wooden grain of grief.
She lets him go.

She cradles his flesh
and calls down the wind,
sings empires down into dust.
She takes his broken mass,
lays him to rest;
her fingers smell of spice.
She breaks and breathes.

She stands to pray,
to summon the dawn,
to shake the sea and the earth.
She signs the coming gift
with priestly hands,
wilding the world and time.
She consecrates.

She pondered all these Things

The blue-silver star
lowers over the salt sea.
She seeks out the deep
deep places of the world
where soft bodies drink in tears
and secrete shells to endure
the crush of pressure.

On the shipwrecked earth,
a woman's eye blurs, focuses,
gathers into its black pupil
the secret treasure it sees;
the dark passageway
that leads to the heart
and what remains unseen.

She absorbs, looks deep,
watches her son's growing,
noting his fragility.
His body is all things;
she guards it well.
She contemplates his gaze,
makes a study of unfeigned love.

She ponders, mind unbowed
by poverty or shame.
See her: a queen going out
to engage her demons
armed with song and wonder;
her feet bathed in the dust
that falls from summer stars.

Assumption

When we left the garden
we mistook certainty for wisdom,
staring for seeing,
owning for loving.

The eye of the ego
refused the gift and gravity of earth,
saw only raw materials
and bodies to control.

We fell away from the ground of being,
we made a disembodied hell.
For paradise is a garden
and a garden needs the earth.

Mary does not sever
what belongs in love together.
She is one and whole
in her birthing of the Word.

She is not weightless;
she knows stretch marks and sighs.
She sings with all her might,
dances with the Spirit.

What is assumed is healed, is known, is shared;
and we are loved for all we are.
For paradise has a new queen
and she dances on the earth.

Black Madonna

No power defines me
No man alive crowned me
They coloured in the lines
But I crossed over them
Now my name is my name

Your shaming won't stain me
Immaculate my skin
No Herod will rule me
No Egypt will hold me
Whose side are you on now?

You keep your inclusion
The box drawn to catch me
I'm queen of the high stars
Ark of the broken stones
You can dance to my song

I'm looking right at you
Have you ever seen me?
Do you look right through me?
I'm icon not idol
My God is in my flesh

Facing the police line
While they snuff out my son
He travelled his own way
They met him with gallows
He's breathing his last breath

No room in the white house
I'm rising with grace now
I'll break all the prisons
Tread down the serpent's head
Held high by God's black hand

She rises

She rises with the dawn
into light limitless,
infinite and immanent.

And with her rise
our wholly human flesh,
our hidden soul's depths,
our stumbling prayers
and speechless wonder.

And with her rise
the way she answered angels
and sang down thrones;
lines creasing a dark face,
stretch marks and scars.

And with her rise
the road into exile,
the shaming of women,
the threat of violence
that never stopped her walk.

And with her rise
the carnality of grace
coming to birth in us;
the song of all creation,
becoming all divine.